The Miracles of Jesus

Retold by

Christopher Rawson
and The Revd. R. H. Lloyd
Chaplain of the Dragon School, Oxford

Illustrated by

Victor Ambrus

D0841837

Nihil obstat Anton Cowan *Censor*
Imprimatur Rt. Rev. David Konstant, V.G., M.A.,
Bishop in Central London

The Wedding in Cana

One day, not long after Jesus began to teach people about God, he and his disciples were asked to go to a wedding in the village of Cana, in Galilee. When they arrived, Jesus was delighted to see his mother, Mary, among the guests.

After the wedding ceremony, everyone was invited to a feast in the bridegroom's house, which his parents had been preparing for many weeks.

The tables were piled high with food, and the servants were busy making sure that everyone had plenty to eat and that their cups were filled with wine. The steward of the feast proposed the first toast to the health and happiness of the bride and bridegroom.

It was a happy party and everyone had plenty to eat and drink.

Then, halfway through the feast, when all the guests were ready to stay for several more hours, one of the servants told the bridegroom's mother that nearly all the wine had been drunk.

The bridegroom's mother was most upset. If there was no more wine, everyone would leave and the family would be very embarrassed. People would talk about it for years.

Mary saw that the bridegroom's mother was worried and followed her out of the room. "What is the matter?" she asked. "All the wine has been drunk," wept the mother. "The wedding is ruined."

Mary comforted her as much as she could. Then she said, "Dry your tears. I know someone who will be able to help you. Go back to your guests and pretend that all is well."

Hurrying through the crowded courtyard to Jesus, Mary told him about the wine. "I thought something was wrong when I saw that the servants had stopped serving it," replied Jesus.

"The bridegroom's mother is so upset. Is there anything you can do to help her?" asked Mary. "But, Mother, what do you expect me to do?" asked Jesus, smiling.

Mary looked at him for a moment, then she smiled. Turning to one of the servants, she said, "Whatever this man tells you to do, you must do."

When she had gone, Jesus pointed to six large water jars standing near the door. "Fill those jars with water from the well as quickly as you can," he said.

"But, Master," stammered the servant, "it is wine we need, not water." Jesus smiled and replied, "You heard what my Mother said. You must do as I tell you."

With a puzzled frown, the servant hurried away to fetch fresh water from the village well. Soon he had filled all the six jars to the brim.

By the time he had finished, many of the guests were calling for more wine. Pointing to the water jars, Jesus told the servants to fill the empty cups.

The servants stared at him in surprise. "But, Master," exclaimed one of them, "we can't give them water!" Jesus said quietly, "Just do as I tell you."

Soon the wedding feast was going well again and the bridegroom's mother talked happily to her guests as they sipped their refilled cups.

As they did so, they started to comment to one another on the fine quality of the wine. The steward of the feast was so impressed that he held up his hand and called for silence.

"Listen to me," he shouted. "I have been to many wedding feasts and at every one the best wine has always been served at the beginning and the cheaper wine kept until everyone has had plenty to drink. But at this feast, the best wine has been served at the end. I would like to thank the bridegroom and his family for such a lovely surprise."

Mary looked across the crowded courtyard and smiled at Jesus. This was the first miracle that he performed.

Feeding Five Thousand People

As Jesus travelled from village to village, more and more people heard news of him. Wherever he went, large crowds gathered to listen as he taught them how they should believe in God.

Sometimes, he went off alone with his disciples so that he could have time to think and pray. One day, he asked his disciples to take him to a quiet place on the other side of Lake Galilee.

The people who saw him go noted which way the boat went across the lake and set off to walk to the place where they knew they would find him.

As they passed through the little fishing villages, the news that Jesus was near spread quickly, and soon more and more people joined the crowd.

7

After a long walk, the crowds of followers came to the place where the disciples had pulled the boat up on the shore. Climbing up the hill, they found Jesus sitting down with his disciples.

When the disciples saw the crowds coming, they were angry. "Why can't they leave Jesus in peace for one day?" they muttered to each other.

Turning to Jesus, they suggested that he should send the people away. But Jesus knew how far many of them had walked to hear him and did not agree.

The crowd grew and grew until there were about five thousand people altogether. They sat down and waited patiently for Jesus to speak to them.

He taught them about God for many hours. When he had finished, he was about to tell them to go home when he realized that they had not eaten all day. Because many of the people had travelled a long way, he felt that he could not send them away hungry.

Turning to Philip, the disciple nearest to him, Jesus asked, "Where can we buy food for all these people?"

Philip shook his head. "Even if we had enough money, there is nowhere here to buy food," he said.

A small boy, sitting nearby, heard what they said. Going up to Andrew, one of the disciples, he said, "I have a picnic which I am ready to share with everyone." Taking hold of the boy's hand, Andrew led him to Jesus.

"Master," Andrew said to Jesus, "this boy has offered to share his picnic with the crowd." Jesus looked at the boy, smiled and asked, "Are you really offering your picnic to us?" "Yes, Master," said the boy, holding it out.

Taking the picnic from the boy, Jesus spoke to the people again. "Listen to me," he said. "I have been telling you that it is God's wish that you should all love one another. This boy has offered to share his picnic with you. Clearly he has understood my teaching." Jesus then blessed the food in the boy's picnic basket, which was just five barley loaves and two small fish.

Then Jesus began to break the bread and fish into pieces. Calling his disciples, he asked them to give the food out to all the people.

He told them to make sure that no one who had come to listen to his teaching went away without something to eat.

When everyone had eaten as much as they wanted, Jesus told them that it was time for them to go home. After they had all gone, Jesus asked his disciples to fetch baskets from the boat.

Picking up all the left-over bits of food, they filled twelve baskets with it. So Jesus had fed a crowd of five thousand people with just one small boy's picnic and there was still lots left over.

Jesus Cures a Leper

At the time of Jesus, the disease called leprosy was so dreaded by the Jews that anyone with it was not allowed to go into the Temple, into the city of Jerusalem or any walled town.

Everyone with the disease, which attacks a person's face, hands, feet and skin, had to leave their homes and live alone in the wilderness.

No one was allowed by law to stand nearer to a leper than twenty paces. And if the wind was blowing from the leper towards another person, the leper had to stand at least 150 paces away.

Lepers had to wear torn clothes and shout, "Unclean! unclean!" whenever they saw someone coming near them.

There was a farmer who lived with his wife and children near the village of Magdala. He worked hard and was a good husband and father.

One evening, when he was washing himself in the stream near his house after a long day's work, he noticed a small white patch on his skin.

12

Later, when his children were asleep, he showed the mark to his wife. She looked at it and whispered, "You must go and have it examined by the priest in case it is leprosy. It would be terrible if the children caught it."

Next day, the farmer went to the priest. After examining the white mark, the priest told him gravely that it was leprosy. "You must leave your home and family," he said, "and go away and live on your own in the wilderness."

The farmer went home and, standing at a safe distance, told his wife the terrible news. Then, after saying goodbye, he went into the lonely countryside.

After several years, the white mark on the man's skin had spread and the disease become worse, attacking his face, his hands and his feet.

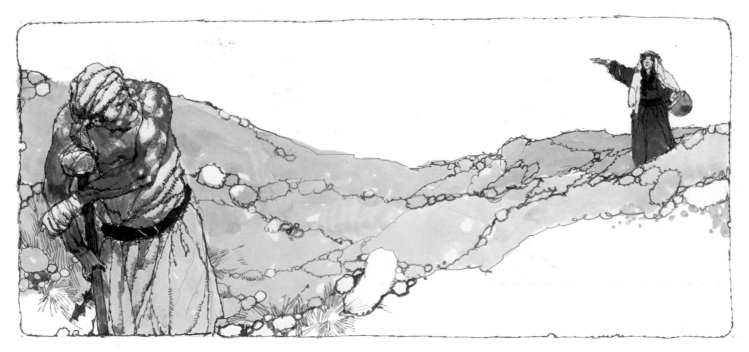

One day the farmer's wife, who had been searching for her husband for a long time, found him on a hillside. She shouted to him that she had heard talk of a kind man, called Jesus, who had the power to cure sick people.

"I heard that he is in this part of the country now," she said. "You will recognise him because he always has twelve followers with him. He seems to be able to heal all sorts of diseases. He might be able to cure you."

A few days later, the farmer saw Jesus coming and, walking to the road, knelt down and waited. When Jesus and his disciples saw him, they stopped in surprise for they knew that lepers were forbidden to go near other people.

"Master!" cried the farmer. "If you care to, you could cure me. Please help me." Peter and the other disciples were afraid of catching the dreaded disease. But Jesus turned to them and told them not to be frightened.

14

Then, to their amazement, Jesus walked up to the leper and put his arms round him. "Of course I want to help you. Be clean," he said. The disciples were horrified that Jesus had put himself in danger of catching leprosy.

But when Jesus took his arms away from the leper, all signs of the disease had disappeared. Jesus said to him gently, "You must now go back to the priest and ask him to declare you cured. Afterwards, you may return home."

The priest examined the farmer carefully and then handed him a certificate to show that he had been cured and was no longer a leper.

The farmer hurried home happily to his wife and family. They were all amazed and overjoyed when he told them of the miracle Jesus had performed for him.

Blind Bartimaeus

Whenever Jesus travelled from Galilee to Jerusalem to celebrate one of the Festivals in the Temple, he stayed at Jericho before starting the long climb up to the city.

Even when it was time for him to leave, the crowds who had been listening to Jesus, did not want to let him go. They would follow him down the streets, asking questions and hoping he would stop to tell them more stories.

As so often happened in other places, a crowd soon gathered round him, asking him to teach them about God.

One day, there was a blind man, called Bartimaeus, sitting near the city gate, begging for money. When he heard the crowd coming, he asked people near him what the noise was all about. They told him that it was Jesus of Nazareth, followed by a large crowd.

As the crowd came nearer, Bartimaeus began to call out, "Jesus, Son of David, have pity on me. Jesus, Son of David, have pity on me." The people near Bartimaeus told him to be quiet. "You can't expect someone as famous as Jesus to bother with you. Be quiet," they said.

Bartimaeus took no notice of them and shouted even louder, "Jesus, Son of David, have pity on me!" When Jesus heard someone shouting his name, he stopped and asked, "Who is calling me?"

One of the people who had tried to silence Bartimaeus said, "It's no one really, Master, only Blind Bartimaeus."

Jesus said, "Bring the man to me." So Bartimaeus was led to Jesus, who asked him gently, "What would you like me to do for you?"

"Master," said Bartimaeus, "please make me able to see again."

Jesus went up to Bartimaeus and, putting his fingers on the blind man's eyes, said, "Because you believe that I can cure you, I give you your sight."

When Jesus took his hands away, Bartimaeus slowly opened his eyes. He looked round him and realised he could see everything that was going on.

For a moment, he was speechless, hardly daring to believe it. Then he raised his arms and shouted with joy, "I can see, I can see! Do you hear me? I can see, I can see again."

Then Bartimaeus, falling to his knees in front of Jesus, thanked him for giving him back his sight. And all the people who had seen Jesus perform this miracle, followed him, praising God.

19

The Paralysed Man

Capernaum was a busy fishing town on the northern shore of Lake Galilee. Jesus spent a lot of time there, teaching and healing the people.

In Capernaum lived a man who was paralysed and could not walk. He had four friends who went to his house each evening and carried him on a stretcher to the town well where people gathered to gossip and exchange news.

One evening, everyone was talking about Jesus. One man said, "Have you heard that Jesus is staying in Simon Peter's house?"

Another man said, "I was told by Andrew that he saw Jesus heal a leper."

A third said, "I heard that he changed water into wine at a wedding."

Then someone added that Jesus was going to tell one of his stories in Simon Peter's house next day.

Later that evening, as the four men carried their friend home, one of them had an idea. "Why don't we take him along to see Jesus tomorrow? Perhaps he would cure him too. If Jesus can heal a leper, I don't see why he can't cure a paralysed man." The four men agreed that it was worth trying and decided to meet at their friend's house the following morning.

Next day, when they carried the man to Peter's house, they found such a huge crowd round it, they could not even get anywhere near the door.

One of the friends asked the people to stand aside and let them in. But they were listening so intently to what Jesus was saying that they did not hear him.

One of the friends noticed that the house had an outside staircase leading up to the flat roof. "Let's go up there," he said. "Perhaps we can find a way in."

They put the stretcher down on the roof and one of the men said to another, "Go and find four pieces of rope and bring them here as quickly as you can."

The other three men drew out the knives which they always carried and began to hack a hole in the roof, right above where Jesus was sitting.

When the fourth man returned with the rope, they tied a piece to each corner of the stretcher and lowered their friend down at Jesus' feet.

When the stretcher reached the floor, Jesus looked at the paralysed man and asked quietly, "My son, what do you want me to do?"

The man replied, "Master, please give me the use of my legs."

Jesus saw how much faith the man and his friends had, and said, "My son, your sins are forgiven."

Jesus noticed that some people in the crowd were frowning with disapproval. They believed that only God could forgive sins; they did not realise that Jesus was the Son of God.

Turning to them, Jesus asked if they would have preferred him just to tell the man to pick up his stretcher and walk. When they did not reply, he smiled at the man who was still lying down and said, "Rise, pick up your bed and walk."

23

Immediately the paralysed man felt the strength and feeling coming back into his useless legs.

Putting his trust in Jesus, he slowly got to his feet, picked up his stretcher and took a few steps.

As the crowd moved aside to let him through, he walked out of the door to his four friends who had come down from the roof and hugged him joyfully.

Behind him, the people who had watched the miracle talked excitedly to one another. They had never seen or heard anything like it before.

Storm on Lake Galilee

One evening, after Jesus had been teaching crowds of followers all day, he wanted to be alone for a while. So he asked his disciples to take him across Lake Galilee to the other side.

Some of the disciples had been fishermen and were able to borrow a boat. Climbing aboard and raising the sail, they were soon skimming across the water. Jesus lay down in the boat and quickly fell asleep.

Suddenly a fierce wind blew up. This often happens on Lake Galilee and can be very dangerous because the wind, blowing down the steep valleys around the lake, can be strong and unexpected.

The wind, quickly changing direction, whips up huge, tumbling waves which can swamp small boats, even those sailed by experienced fishermen. It was such a storm which broke when Jesus and his disciples were crossing the lake.

Then the rain began to lash down and the waves, whipped up by the gale, crashed into the boat.

The disciples swiftly lowered the sail before the mast snapped, and grabbed the oars to try to row the boat and keep it under control.

But the waves broke over the sides and they began to sink lower and lower in the water. The disciples were terrified, expecting to capsize at any moment.

All through the noise of the roaring storm and lashing rain, Jesus still slept peacefully in the boat.

At last, panic-stricken, Peter shook Jesus by the shoulder and shouted above the wind, "Master, the boat is sinking and we will all drown. Save us!"

Jesus awoke and looked around him. Standing up, he raised his hands and spoke to the wind and waves, "Hush, be still," he said.

The disciples looked at one another in astonishment. "Who can this be?" they asked. "He gives orders to the wind and waves, and even they obey him."

At once, the wind began to drop and the lake became calm again. Jesus said to his disciples, "Why are you such cowards? Have you no faith, even now?"

Jairus' daughter

One of the most important men in the town of Capernaum was Jairus, who was the President of the synagogue. He lived in a fine house with his wife and twelve-year-old daughter.

The little girl had caught a disease and was very ill. Jairus called in all the doctors in the town, but none of them could do anything to make her better. The girl became worse and worse.

One day a friend of Jairus called at the house and peeped into the girl's room where she was lying in bed.

"Listen, Jairus," he said. "I have just walked across the town square. I saw Jesus there, talking to a large crowd of people. Why don't you go and ask him to help. If he can make a paralysed man walk and heal a leper, surely he will be able to cure your daughter."

Taking his friend's advice, Jairus set off immediately for the town square, which was not far away.

When he arrived, Jairus found Jesus completely surrounded by a large crowd, listening to his teaching.

Pushing his way through the crowd, Jairus went up to Jesus and knelt down in front of him. "My daughter is dying," cried Jairus. "I beg you to come home with me and save her life."

"Of course I will come," Jesus replied gently. "Take me to your daughter." As Jesus followed Jairus, the people pressed round them so that they had to push their way through the crowd.

Amongst the people listening to Jesus was a woman who had been ill for twelve years. Although she had spent a lot of money on doctors and medicines, she had not found a cure.

She said to herself, "If only I could touch the edge of Jesus' clothes, I am sure I would be healed."

As Jesus passed near her, she stretched out her hand. The moment she touched the edge of his cloak, she felt a power flowing through her and immediately knew she was cured. Jesus stopped and, looking round, asked, "Who touched me?"

One of his disciples replied, "How can you ask who touched you, when so many people are pressing round you?"

Jesus looked at Peter and said, "Someone touched me deliberately. I felt the power going out from me."

When the woman realized that she had been healed, she knelt at Jesus' feet and admitted what she had done.

Jesus looked down at her and said, "My daughter, your faith has cured you. Go in peace. You are cured for ever of your illness."

As they came near Jairus' house, a man ran up to them and cried, "Jairus, you are too late. Your daughter is dead. There is no point in bringing Jesus now."

Jairus stopped and stared at the man. Then he broke down and wept. Jesus, putting his arm round Jarius, said, "Don't be afraid. Have faith."

They went into the house together and found many people mourning for the girl. When Jesus saw them, he said, "Why are you all weeping like this? The child is not dead. She is only sleeping."

When they heard what Jesus said, the people stopped weeping and laughed scornfully at him. Jesus ordered them all out of the house and gently asked Jairus to take him to his daughter.

Jairus led Jesus into his daughter's room where she was lying on her bed. Her mother, her head bowed in grief, was standing beside her.

Walking up to the bed, Jesus took hold of the girl's hand and said quietly, "Get up, my child." At once, the girl opened her eyes and looked at him.

As they watched, she got up off her bed and walked across the room. Turning to Jairus and his wife, Jesus said, "I think your daughter is hungry and would like something to eat now."

So Jesus left Capernaum and continued to teach the people about God and to heal them, until the time came for his last journey to Jerusalem.